THE CASE AGAINST RELIGION:
A Psychotherapist's View

and

THE CASE AGAINST RELIGIOSITY

by
Albert Ellis
Ph.D.

Introduction by Jon G. Murray

American Atheist Press
Cranford, New Jersey

ISBN10: 0910309-18-3
ISBN13: 978-0910309-18-9

© 1976, 2010 American Atheist Press
P.O. Box 158
Cranford, N.J. 07016
www.atheists.org

Introduction

Albert Ellis is one of the leading sexologist-psychotherapists in the world. Because of his expertise in this area, in puritan United States, he has been both censored and denied the popular recognition he deserves. His impeccable credentials are of no avail *vis-à-vis* the fundamentalist religion and the reactionary politics which have dominated our nation in the last decade. Although he is well known to and acclaimed by the professionals in his field, he has not become the folk hero he should be.

Ellis was born in Pittsburgh, Pennsylvania on September 27, 1913. He received his B.B.A. from City College, New York in 1934, his M.A. in 1943, and his Ph.D. in 1974 from Columbia University. In 1948 his career started in the northern New Jersey Mental Hygiene Clinic and by the next year he was the chief psychologist at the Diagnostic Center, in Menlo Park. By 1950 he was the chief psychologist of the New Jersey Dept. of Human Services. However, he has always maintained his own private practice in psychotherapy. In 1959 he founded the new psychotherapeutic method of Rational Emotive Psychotherapy and became the executive director of the Institute for Rational Living, a position which he still holds. He has been the Executive Director of the Institute of Advanced Study in Rational Psychotherapy since 1968, a professor of psychology at Rutgers University since 1973. He is a member of the American Psychological Association (division of consulting psychology,) past president of both Social Science Study of Sex, and American Academy of Psychotherapists, past vice president, National Council on Family Relations, past chairman, division of marriage counseling; past board of directors

American Association of Marriage and Family Counselors, and past executive council, New York Society of Clinical Psychologists. He is a fellow of the American Sociological Association, of the American Psychological Association, the American Association for the Advance of Science, and of the American Anthropological Association. He is a Diplomate in American Board of Examiners in Professional Psychology, and Vice President American Academy of Psychotherapists.

He received the Distinguished Research Award for Social Science Study of Sex in 1971, the Distinguished Professional Psychologist Award, Division of Psychotherapy American Psychological Association in 1974.

His books include: *The Folklore of Sex*, 1951; (with A. P. Phillay) *Sex, Society and The Individual*, 1953; *Sex Life of the American Woman and The Kinsey Report*, 1954; *The American Sexual Tragedy*, 1954; (with Ralph Brancale) *The Psychology of Sex Offenders*, 1956; *How to Live with A Neurotic*, 1957; *Sex without Guilt*, 1958; (with Robert A. Harper) *The Art and Science of Love*, 1960; (with Robert Harper) *A Guide to Rational Living*, 1961; (with Albert Abarbanel) *The Encyclopedia of Sexual Behavior*, 1961; *Creative Marriage*, 1962; *Reason and Emotion in Psychotherapy*, 1962; *If This Be Sexual Heresy...*, 1963; *Sex and The Single Man*, 1963; *The Intelligent Woman's Guide to Manhunting*, 1963; (with Edward Sagarin) *Nymphomania: A Study of the Oversexed Woman*, 1964; (with Ralph Brancale) *The Psychology of Sex Offenders*, 1965; *Suppressed: Seven Essays Publishers Dared Not Print*, 1965; *Sex without Guilt*, 1966; *Art of Erotic Seduction*, 1968; (with John Gallo) *Murder & Assassination*, 1971; *Executive Leadership; A Rational Approach*, 1972; *Sensuous Person: Critique & Corrections*, 1973; *How to Live with — and without — Anger*, 1977; (with Russell Grieger) *Handbook of Rational-Emotive Therapy*, 1977; *Reason and Emotion in Psychotherapy*, 1977; (with Robert A. Harper) *A Guide to Successful Marriage*,

1978; (with William Knaus) *On Overcoming Procrastination*, 1979: *Growth through Reason*, 1980; (with John Whiteley) *Theoretical and Empirical Foundations of Rational-Emotive Therapy*, 1980; (with Janet L. Wolfe) *How to Raise an Emotionally Healthy, Happy Child*, 1981; (with Irving Becker) *Guide to Personal Happiness*, 1982; (with Eliot Abrahms) *Brief Psychotherapy in Medical and Health Practice*, 1983.

Albert Ellis was featured as the principal speaker at the 10th Annual National American Atheist Convention in Chicago, Illinois. At that time, he delivered a speech which he titled, "The Case Against Religion." Subsequently, with his permission, this was brought out as a booklet by American Atheists. Recently Dr. Ellis updated that treatise and both the old and the new are included in this booklet. The old, printed first, begins on page 3; the new, just received, and titled "The Case Against Religiosity" begins on page 21.

In both articles, Dr. Ellis explores the traits necessary to a minimally anxious and hostile individual, and how religion and a belief in a supernatural being eradicate each of these personality traits. Furthermore, Dr. Ellis gives insight into the irrational beliefs held by most seriously disturbed individuals, and shows how religion supports these detrimental beliefs. His basic premise is, "All true believers in any kind of... orthodoxy are distinctly disturbed, since they are obviously rigid, fanatic, and dependent individuals.... Many liberal religionists of various groups are... emotionally childish. For that is what all manner of religion essentially is: childish dependency."

Jon Murray

THE CASE AGAINST RELIGION:
A Psychotherapist's View

by
Albert Ellis
Ph.D.

Before we can talk sensibly about religion — or almost anything else! — we should give some kind of definition of what we are talking about. Let me, therefore, start with what I think are some legitimate definitions of the term *religion*. Other concepts of this term, of course, exist; but what I am talking about when I use it is as follows.

According to *Webster's New Word Dictionary*, religion is: "(1) belief in a divine or superhuman power or powers to be obeyed and worshipped as the creator(s) and ruler(s) of the universe; (2) expression of this belief in conduct and ritual."

English and English, in their *Comprehensive Dictionary of Psychological and Psychoanalytical Terms* (1958), define religion as "a system of beliefs by means of which individuals or a community put themselves in relation to God or to a supernatural world and often to each other, and from which the religious person derives a set of values by which to judge events in the natural world."

The Columbia Encyclopedia notes that "when a man becomes conscious of a power above and beyond the human, and recognizes a dependence of himself upon that power, religion has become a factor in his being."

These, then are the definitions of religion which I accept and which I shall have in mind as I discuss the religious viewpoint in this paper. Religion, to me, must include some concept of a deity. When the term is used merely to denote a system of beliefs, practices, or ethical values which are not connected with any assumed higher power, then I believe it is used loosely and confusingly; since such a non-supernatural system of beliefs can more accurately be described as a philosophy of life or a code of ethics, and it is misleading to confuse a believer in this general kind of philosophy or ethical code with a true religionist.

Every Atheist, in other words, has some kind of philosophy and some code of ethics; and many Atheists, in fact, have much more rigorous life philosophies and ethical systems than have most deists.

SOMEONE IS RELIGIOUS

It therefore seems silly to say that someone is religious because he happens to be philosophic or ethical; and unless we rigorously use the term religion to mean some kind of faith unfounded on fact, or dependency on some assumed superhuman entities, we broaden the definition of the word so greatly as to make it practically meaningless.

If religion is defined as man's dependence on a power above and beyond the human, then, as a psychotherapist, I find it to be exceptionally pernicious. For the psychotherapist is normally dedicated to helping human beings in general, and his patients in particular, to achieve certain goals of mental health, and virtually all these goals are antithetical to a truly religious viewpoint.

Let us look at the main psychotherapeutic goals. On the basis of twenty years of clinical experience, and in basic agreement with most of my professional colleagues (such as Brasten, 1961; Dreikurs, 1955; Fromm, 1955; Goldstein, 1954; Maslow, 1954, Rogers, 1957; and Thorne, 1961), I would say that the psychotherapist tries to help his patients to be minimally anxious and hostile; and to this end, he tries to help them to acquire the following kind of personality traits:

1. *Self-interest*. The emotionally healthy individual should primarily be true to himself and not masochistically sacrifice himself for others. His kindness and consideration for others should be derived from the idea that he himself wants to enjoy freedom from unnecessary pain and restriction, and that he is only likely to do so by helping create a world in which the rights of others, as well as his own, are not needlessly curtailed.

2. *Self-direction.* He should assume responsibility for his own life, be able independently to work out most of his problems, and while at times wanting or preferring the cooperation and help of others, not need their support for his effectiveness and well-being.

3. *Tolerance.* He should fully give other human beings the right to be wrong; and while disliking or abhorring some of their behavior, still not blame them, as persons, for performing this dislikable behavior. He should accept the fact that all humans are remarkably fallible, never unrealistically expect them to be perfect, and refrain from despising or punishing them when they make inevitable mistakes and errors.

4. *Acceptance of uncertainty.* The emotionally mature individual should completely accept the fact that we all live in a world of probability and chance, where there are not, nor probably ever will be, any absolute certainties, and should realize that it is not at all horrible, indeed — such a probabilistic, uncertain world.

5. *Flexibility.* He should remain intellectually flexible, be open to change at all times, and unbigotedly view the infinitely varied people, ideas and things in the world around him.

6. *Scientific thinking.* He should be objective, rational and scientific; and be able to apply the laws of logic and of scientific method not only to external people and events, but to himself and his interpersonal relationships.

7. *Commitment.* He should be vitally absorbed in something outside of himself, whether it be people, things, or ideas; and should preferably have at least one major creative interest, as well as some outstanding human involvement, which is highly important to him, and around which he structures a good part of his life.

8. *Risk-taking.* The emotionally sound person should be able to take risks, to ask himself what he would really like to do in life, and then to try to do this, even though he has to risk defeat or failure. He should be adventurous (though not necessarily foolhardy); be willing to try almost anything once, just to see how he likes it; and look forward to some breaks in his usual life routines.

9. *Self-acceptance.* He should normally be glad to be alive, and to like himself just because he is alive because he exists, and because he (as a living being) invariably has some power to enjoy himself to create happiness and joy. He should not equate his worth or value to himself on his extrinsic achievements, or on what others think of him, but on his personal existence; on his ability to think, feel, and act, and thereby to make some kind of an interesting, absorbed life for himself.

These, then, are the kind of personality traits which a psychotherapist is interested in helping his patients achieve and which he is also, prophylactically, interested in fostering in the lives of millions who will never be his patients.

Now, does religion — by which again, I mean faith unfounded on fact, or dependence on some supernatural deity — help human beings to achieve these healthy traits and thereby to avoid becoming anxious, depressed, and hostile?

The answer, of course, is that it doesn't help at all; and in most respects it seriously sabotages mental health. For religion, first of all, is not self-interest; it is god-interest.

The religious person must, by virtual definition, be so concerned with whether or not his hypothesized god loves him, and whether he is doing the right thing to continue to keep in this god's good graces, that he must, at very best, put himself second and must sacrifice some of his most cherished interests to appease this god. If, moreover, he is a member of any organized religion, then he must choose his god's precepts first, those of this church and its clergy second, and his own views and preferences third.

NO VIEWS OF HIS OWN

In a sense, the religious person must have no real views of his own; and it is presumptuous of him, in fact, to have any. In regard to sex-love affairs, to marriage and family relations, to business, to politics, and to virtually everything else that is important in his life, he must try to discover what his god and his clergy would like him to do; and he must primarily do their bidding.

Masochistic self-sacrifice is an integral part of almost all organized religions: as shown, for example, in the various forms of ritualistic self-deprivation that Jews, Christians, Mohammedans, and other religionists must continually undergo if they are to keep in good with their assumed gods.

Masochism, indeed, stems from an individual's deliberately inflicting pain on himself in order that he may guiltlessly permit himself to experience some kind of sexual or other pleasure; and the very essence of most organized religions is the performance of masochistic, guilt-soothing rituals, by which the religious individual gives himself permission to enjoy life.

Religiosity, to a large degree, essentially is masochism; and both are forms of mental sickness.

In regard to self-direction, it can easily be seen from what has just been said that the religious person is by necessity dependent and other-directed rather than independent and self-directed. If he is true to his religious beliefs he must first bow down to his god; second, to the clergy who run this god's church; and third, to all the members of his religious sect, who are eagle-eyedly watching him to see whether he defects an iota from the conduct his god and his church define as proper.

If religion, therefore, is largely masochism, it is even more dependency. For a man to be a true believer and to be strong and independent is impossible; religion and self-sufficiency are contradictory terms.

Tolerance again, is a trait that the firm religionist cannot possibly possess. "I am the Lord thy God and thou shalt have no other gods before me," saith Jehovah. Which means, in plain English, that whatever any given god and his clergy believe must be absolutely, positively true; and whatever any other person or group believes must be absolutely, positively false.

Democracy, permissiveness, and the acceptance of human fallibility are quite alien to the real religionist — since he can only believe that the creeds and commands of his particular deity should, ought and must be obeyed, and that anyone who disobeys them is patently a knave.

Religion, with its definitional absolutes, can never rest with the concept of an individual's wrongdoing or making mistakes, but must inevitably add to this the notion of his sinning and of his deserving to be punished for his sins. For, if it is merely desirable for you to refrain from harming others or committing other misdeeds, as any non-religious code of ethics will inform you that it is, then if you make a mistake and do commit some misdeeds, you are merely a wrongdoer, or one who is doing an undesirable deed and who should try to correct himself and do less wrong in the future. But if it is god-given, absolutistic law that you shall not, must not do a wrong act, and actually do it, you are then a mean, miserable sinner, a worthless being, and must severely punish yourself (perhaps eternally, in hell) for being a wrongdoer, being a fallible human.

Religion, then, by setting up absolute, god-given standards, must make you self-depreciating and dehumanized when you err; and must lead you to despise and dehumanize others when they act badly. This kind of absolutistic, perfectionistic thinking is the prime creator of the two most corroding of human emotions: anxiety and hostility.

If one of the requisites for emotional health is acceptance of uncertainty, then religion is obviously the unhealthiest state imaginable: since its prime reason for being is to enable the religionist to believe in a mystical certainty.

Just because life is so uncertain, and because millions of people think that they cannot take its vicissitudes, they invent absolutistic gods, and thereby pretend that there is some final, invariant answer to things. Patently, these people are fooling themselves — and instead of healthfully admitting that they do not need certainty, but can live comfortably in this often disorderly world, they stubbornly protect their neurotic beliefs by insisting that there must be the kind of certainty that they foolishly believe that they need.

This is like a child's believing that he must have a kindly father in order to survive; and then, when his father is unkindly, or perhaps has died and is nonexistent, he dreams up a father (who may be a neighbor, a movie star, or a pure figment of his imagination) and he insists that this dream-father actually exists.

The trait of flexibility, which is so essential to proper emotional functioning, is also blocked and sabotaged by religious belief. For the person who dogmatically believes in god, and who sustains this belief with a faith unfounded in fact, which a true religionist of course must, clearly is not open to change and is necessarily bigoted.

If, for example, his scriptures or his church tell him that he shalt not even covet his neighbor's wife — let alone have actual adulterous relations with her! — he cannot ask himself, "Why should I not lust after this woman, as long as I don't intend to do anything about my desire for her? What is really wrong about that?" For his god and his church have spoken; and there is no appeal from this arbitrary authority, once he has brought himself to accept it.

Any time, in fact, anyone unempirically establishes a god or a set of religious postulates which have a superhuman origin, he can thereafter use no empirical evidence whatever to question the dictates of this god or those postulates, since they are (by definition) beyond scientific validation.

The best he can do, if he wants to change any of the rules that stem from his religion, is to change the religion itself. Otherwise, he is stuck with the absolutistic axioms, and their logical corollaries, that he himself has initially accepted on faith. We may therefore note again that, just as religion is masochism, other-directedness, intolerance, and refusal to accept uncertainty, it also is mental and emotional inflexibility.

In regard to scientific thinking, it practically goes without saying that this kind of cerebration is quite antithetical to religiosity. The main canon of the scientific method — as Ayer (1947), Carnap (1953), Reichenbach (1953), and a host of other modern philosophers of science have pointed out — is that, at least in some final analysis, or in principle, all theories be confirmable by some form of human experience, some empirical referent. But all religions which are worthy of the name contend that their superhuman entities cannot be seen, heard, smelled, tasted, felt, or otherwise humanly experienced, and that their gods and their principles are therefore distinctly beyond science.

To believe in any of these religions, therefore, is to be unscientific at least to some extent; and it could well be contended that the more religious one is, the less scientific one tends to be. Although a religious person need not be entirely unscientific (as, for that matter, a raving maniac need not be either), it is difficult to see how he could be perfectly scientific.

While a person may be both scientific and religious (as he may also be at times sensible and at other times foolish) it is doubtful if an individual's attitude may simultaneously be truly pious and objective.

In regard to the trait of commitment, the religious individual may — for once! — have some advantages. For if he is truly religious, he is seriously committed to his god, his church, or his creed; and to some extent, at least, he thereby acquires a major interest in life.

Religious commitment also frequently has its serious disadvantages, since it tends to be obsessive-compulsive; and it may well interfere with other kinds of healthy commitments — such as deep involvements in sex-love relations, in scientific pursuits, and even in artistic endeavors. Moreover, it is a commitment that is often motivated by guilt or hostility, and may serve as a frenzied covering-up mechanism which masks, but does not really eliminate, these underlying disturbed feelings. It is also the kind of commitment that is based on falsehoods and illusions, and that therefore easily can be shattered, thus plunging the previously committed individual into the depths of disillusionment and despair.

Not all forms of commitment, in other words, are equally healthy. The grand inquisitors of the medieval catholic church were utterly dedicated to their "holy" work, and Hitler and many of his associates were fanatically committed to their Nazi doctrines. But this hardly proves that they are emotionally stable human beings.

When religious individuals are happily committed to faith, they often tend to be fanatically and dogmatically committed in an obsessive compulsive way that itself is hardly desirable. Religious commitment may well be better for a human being than no commitment to anything. But religion, to a large degree, is fanaticism — which, in turn, is an obsessive-compulsive, rigid form of holding to a viewpoint that invariably masks and provides a bulwark for the underlying insecurity of the obsessed individual.

In regard to risk-taking, it should be obvious that the religious person is highly determined not to be adventurous nor to take any of life's normal risks. He strongly believes in unvalidatable assumptions precisely because he does not want to risk following his own preferences and aims, but wants the guarantee that some higher power will back him.

Enormously fearing failure, and falsely defining his own worth as a person in terms of achievement, he sacrifices time, energy, and material goods and pleasures to the worship of the assumed god, so that he can at least be sure that this god loves and supports him. All religions worthy of the name are distinctly inhibiting — which means, in effect, that the religious person sells his soul, surrenders his own basic urges and pleasures, so that he may feel comfortable with the heavenly helper that he himself has invented. Religion, then, is needless inhibition.

Finally, in regard to self-acceptance, it should again be clear that the religious devotee cannot possibly accept himself just because he is alive, because he exists and has, by mere virtue of his aliveness, some power to enjoy himself. Rather he must make his self-acceptance utterly contingent on the acceptance of his definitional god, the church and clergy who also serve this god, and all other true believers in his religion.

If all these extrinsic persons and things accept him, he is able — and even then only temporarily and with continued underlying anxiety — to accept himself. Which means, of course, that he defines himself only through the reflected appraisals of others and loses any real, existential self that he might otherwise keep creating. Religion, for such an individual, consequently is self-abasement and self-abnegation — as, of course, virtually all the saints and mystics have clearly stated that it is.

If we summarize what we have just been saying, the conclusion seems inescapable that religion is, on almost every conceivable count, directly opposed to the goals of mental health since it basically consists of masochism, other-directedness, intolerance, refusal to accept uncertainty, unscientific thinking, needless inhibition, and self-abasement. In the one area where religion has some advantage in terms of emotional hygiene — that of encouraging hearty commitment to a cause or project in which the person may be vitally absorbed — it even tends to sabotage this advantage in two important ways: (a) it drives most of its adherents to commit themselves to its tenets for the wrong reasons that is, to cover up instead of to face and rid themselves of their basic insecurities; and (b) it encourages a fanatic, obsessive-compulsive kind of commitment that is, in its own right, a form of mental illness.

If we want to look at the problem of human disturbance a little differently, we may ask ourselves, "What are the irrational ideas which people believe and through which they drive themselves into severe states of emotional sickness?"

EXPLORING THE QUESTION

After exploring this question for many years, and developing a new form of psychotherapy which is specifically directed at quickly unearthing and challenging the main irrational ideas which make people neurotic and psychotic, I have found that these ideas may be categorized under a few major headings (Ellis, 1962; Ellis and Harper, 1961a, 1961b). Here, for example, are five irrational notions, all or some of which are strongly held by practically every seriously disturbed person; here, along with these notions, are the connections between them and commonly held religious beliefs.

Irrational idea No. 1 is the idea that it is a dire necessity for an adult to be loved or approved of by all the significant figures in his life. This idea is bolstered by the religious philosophy that if you cannot get certain people to love or approve of you, you can always fall back on God's love. The thought, however, that it is quite possible for you to live comfortably in the world whether or not other people accept you is quite foreign to both emotionally disturbed people and religionists.

Irrational idea No. 2 is the idea that you must be thoroughly competent, adequate, and achieving in all possible respects, otherwise you are worthless. The religionists say that no, you need not be competent and achieving, and in fact can be thoroughly inadequate — as long as god loves you and you are a member in good standing of the church. But this means, of course, that you must be a competent and achieving religionist — else you are no damned good.

Irrational idea No. 3 is the notion that certain people are bad, wicked, and villainous and that they should be severely blamed and punished for their sins. This is the ethical basis, of course, of virtually all true religions. The concepts of guilt, blaming, and sin are, in fact, almost synonymous with that of revealed religion.

Irrational idea No. 4 is the belief that it is horrible, terrible, and catastrophic when things are not going the way you would like them to go. This idea, again, is the very core of religiosity, since the religious person invariably believes that just because he cannot stand being frustrated, and just because he must keep worrying about things turning out badly, he needs a supreme deity to supervise his thoughts and deeds and to protect him from anxiety and frustration.

Irrational ideal No. 5 is the idea that human unhappiness is externally caused and that people have little or no ability to control their sorrows or rid themselves of their negative feelings. Once again, this notion is the essence of religion, since real religions invariably teach you that only by trusting in God and relying on and praying to him will you be able to control your sorrows or counteract your negative emotions.

Similarly, if we had the time to review all the other major irrational ideas that lead humans to become and to remain emotionally disturbed, we would quickly find that they are coextensive with, or are strongly encouraged by, religious tenets.

If you think about the matter carefully, you will see that this close connection between mental illness and religion is inevitable and invariant, since neurosis or psychosis is something of a high-class name for childishness or dependency; and religion, when correctly used, is little more than a synonym for dependency.

In the final analysis, then, *religion is neurosis*. This is why I remarked, at a symposium on sin and psychotherapy held by the American Psychological Association a few years ago, that from a mental health standpoint Voltaire's famous dictum should be reversed: for if there *were* a god, it would be necessary to uninvent him.

If the thesis of this article is correct, religion goes hand in hand with the basic irrational beliefs of human beings. These keep them dependent, anxious, and hostile, and thereby create and maintain their neuroses and psychoses. What then is the role of psychotherapy in dealing with the religious views of disturbed patients? Obviously, the sane and effective psychotherapist should not — as many contemporary psychoanalytic Jungian, client-centered, and existentialist therapists have contended he should — go along with the patients' religious orientation and try to help these patients live successfully with their religions, for this is equivalent to trying to help them live successfully with their emotional illness.

EXCLUSIVE HOMOSEXUALITY

If a man is fearfully fixated on exclusive homosexuality, or obsessively engaged in hating his boss, or compulsively dependent on the love of his mother, no sensible psychotherapist would try to enable him to retain his crippling neurotic symptoms and still lead a happy life.

The effective therapist, instead, would, of course, try to help this man live successfully without his symptoms — and to this end would keep hammering away at the basic irrational philosophies of life which cause the patient to manufacture and to hang on to his manifestations of emotional illness.

So will the therapist, if he himself is not too sick or gutless, attack his patient's religiosity. Not only will he show this patient that he is religious — meaning, as we previously noted, that he is masochistic, other-directed, intolerant, unable to accept uncertainty, unscientific, needlessly inhibited, self-abasing, and fanatic — but he will also quite vigorously and forcefully question, challenge, and attack the patient's irrational beliefs that support these disturbed traits.

This is what is done in my own system of psychotherapy, which is called rational-emotive psychotherapy. Where other systems of therapy largely try to give the patient insight into the origins of his self-defeating beliefs (as, for example, the Freudians do) or try to help him accept himself with his self-sabotaging behavior (as the existential and client-centered therapists do), in rational therapy we give him insight and accept him in spite of his failings — but we also, and I think more importantly, clearly show him how he keeps maintaining his early-acquired irrationalities by indoctrinating himself over and over with nonsensical internalized sentences which sustain this nonsense; and show him how he can concretely challenge and contradict these internalized philosophies, by logically parsing and analyzing them, and by convincing himself that he must give them up if he is to regain emotional health. Rational-emotive psychotherapy, in other words, goes distinctly beyond the usual insight producing and patient-accepting methods of treatment in that it actively depropagandizes the patient and teaches him how the highly irrational and essentially superstitious and religious beliefs that he acquired from his parents and his culture can be thoroughly combated until they are truly non-existent.

THE DISTURBED INDIVIDUAL

RT, as rational therapy is called for short, literally teaches the disturbed individual how he can apply the methods of scientific thinking to himself and his personal relationships with others; and it usually does so with many fewer sessions of psychotherapy than the more conventional psychoanalytic and other schools use. It is, however, an unusually depth-centered and thoroughgoing form of treatment, in that it is not interested in symptom removal or in release of feelings, but in an extensive and intensive reorganization of the patient's basic philosophy of life. While valuing the patient himself and his inalienable, existential right to happiness, it vigorously and most directly attacks his self-sabotaging values and his self-repeated irrational internal verbalizations which uphold these. This is not the place to give the details of the theory and practice of rational-emotive psychotherapy, since they may be found in my book *Reason and Emotion in Psychotherapy*.

Not that RT is the only method of helping human beings to change their fundamental irrational and superstitious ideas about themselves, others, and the world. Various other depropagandizing techniques, including books, lectures, and works of literature, as well as other modes of psychotherapy, can also be most useful in this respect. The main point it, however, that the vast majority of people in contemporary society are basically irrational and religious in their thinking and feeling — and hence are more or less emotionally sick. All true believers in any kind of orthodoxy whether it be religious, political, social, or even artistic orthodoxy — are distinctly disturbed, since they are obviously rigid, fanatic, and dependent individuals (Hoffer, 1951). And many liberal religionists of various groups are distinctly less, but still quite definitely, emotionally childish. For that, again, is what all manner of religion essentially is: childish dependency. And that is what effective psychotherapy, along with all the other healing arts and informative sciences, must continue uncompromisingly to unmask and eradicate.

REFERENCES

Ayer, A.J., *Language, Truth and Logic*. New York: Dover Publications, 1947.

Brasten, Leif J., "The Main Theories of Existentialism from the Viewpoint of a Psycho-therapist." *Mental Hygiene*, 1961 (45) 10–17.

Carnap, Rudolf, "Testability and Meaning." In Feigl, H., and M. Brodbeck, eds., *Readings in the Philosophy of Science*. New York: Appleton-Century-Crofts, 1953.

Dreikurs, Rudolf, *The Adlerian Approach on the Changing Scope of Psychiatry*. Chicago: author, 1955.

Ellis, Albert, *Reason and Emotion in Psychotherapy*. New York: Lyle Stuart, 1962.

Ellis, Albert and Robert A. Harper, *A Guide to Rational Living*. Englewood-Cliffs, N.J.: Prentice-Hall, 1961.

Fromm, Erich, *The Sane Society*, New York: Rinehart, 1955.

Hoffer, Eric, *The True Believer*, New York: Harper, 1951.

Maslow, A.H., *Motivation and Personality*, New York: Harper, 1954.

Reichenbach, Hans, "The Verifiability Theory of Meaning." In Feigl, H., and M. Brodbeck, eds., *Readings in the Philosophy of Science*. New York: Appleton-Century-Crofts, 1953.

Rogers, Carl R. "The Necessary and Sufficient Conditions of Therapeutic Personality Change," *Journal of Consulting Psychology*, 1957 (21) 459–461.

THE CASE AGAINST RELIGIOSITY

by
Albert Ellis
Ph.D.

This article will try to make a succinct and cogent case for the proposition that unbelief, skepticism, and thoroughgoing Atheism not only abet but are practically synonymous with mental health; and that devout belief, dogmatism, and religiosity distinctly contribute to and in some ways are equal to mental or emotional disturbance. The case against religiosity that I am about to make is, of course, hardly unassailable and is only presented as a firm (and undevout!) hypothesis that I believe has validity but that (like all scientific hypotheses) is tentative and revisable in the light of later substantiating or non-substantiating evidence. I shall try to state it so that, as Karl Popper has advocated, it is falsifiable and therefore scientific.

Before I attempt to write about the advantages and disadvantages of devout religion (or religiosity), let me try to clearly define these terms. Traditionally, the term religion has meant some kind of belief in the supernatural. Thus, *Webster's New World Dictionary* defines religion as: "(1) belief in a divine or superhuman power or powers to be obeyed and worshipped as the creator(s) and ruler(s) of the universe; (2) expression of this belief in conduct and ritual." However, in recent years religion has also come to be defined in broader terms than this; so that the same dictionary continues: "(3) Any specific system of belief, worship, conduct, *etc.*, often 1 involving a code of ethics and a philosophy: as, the Christian religion, the Buddhist religion, *etc.* Loosely, any system of beliefs, practices, ethical values, *etc.* resembling, suggestive of, or likened to such a system: as, humanism is his religion."

In the following article, I shall mainly discuss two particular forms of devout religion or religiosity. The first of these is a devout or orthodox belief in some kind of supernatural religion, such as Judaism, Christianity, or Mohammedanism — or pious adherence to the kind of religion mentioned in Webster's first two definitions. The second form of religiosity I shall discuss is a devout or rigid belief in some kind of secular religion (such as Libertarianism, Marxism, or Freudianism) — that is, a dogmatic, absolutistic conviction that some political, economic, social, or philosophic view is sacrosanct, provides ultimate answers to virtually all important questions, and is to be piously subscribed to and followed by everyone who wishes to lead a good life.

I shall not, then, particularly discuss Webster's third definition of religion, since when the term is used to denote a mild system of beliefs, practices, or ethical values that are not connected with any assumed higher power, and that are not believed in absolutistic ally, devoutly, or dogmatically by secular religionists, I do not think that this kind of "religion" leads to any special individual or social harm. So a *vague, general,* or *moderate* set of "religious" beliefs will not be scrutinized in this article; but only a *devout* and *pious* brand of religiosity. Stated a little differently: I shall not attempt to relate absolutistic *religiosity* rather than mild *religion* to the existence of mental and emotional health.

Although no group of authorities fully agree on a definition of the term *mental health*, it seems to include several traits and behaviors that are frequently endorsed by leading theorists and therapists. I have outlined the desirability of these "healthy" traits in several of my writings on rational-emotive therapy (RET) and they have also been generally endorsed by many other therapists, including Sigmund Freud, Carl Jung, Alfred Adler, Karen Horney, Erich Fromm, Rudolf Dreikurs, Fritz Perls, Abraham Maslow, Marie Jahoda, Carl Rogers, and Rollo May. These include such traits as self-interest, self-direction, social interest, tolerance, acceptance of ambiguity, acceptance of reality, commitment, risk-taking, self-acceptance, rationality, and scientific thinking. Not all mentally healthy individuals possess the highest degree of these traits at all times. But when people seriously lack them or when they have extreme opposing behaviors, we often consider them to be at least somewhat emotionally disturbed.

Assuming that the above criteria for mental health and a few other related criteria are reasonably valid, how are they sabotaged by a system of devout religious belief or religiosity? And how are they abetted by adherence to the principles of unbelief, skepticism, and Atheism? Let us now consider these questions.

1. *Self-interest.* Emotionally healthy people are primarily true to themselves and do not masochistically subjugate themselves to or unduly sacrifice themselves for others. They tend to put themselves first — realizing that if they do not primarily take care of themselves, who else will ? — as well as put a few selected others a close second and the rest of the world not too far behind.

Rather than be primarily self-interested, devout deity-oriented religionists put their hypothesized god(s) first and themselves second — or last! They are so over concerned whether their god loves them, and whether they are doing the right thing to continue in this god's good graces, that they sacrifice some of their most cherished and enjoyable interest to supposedly appease this god. If, moreover, they are a member of any orthodox church or organization, they feel forced to choose their god's precepts first, those of their church or organization second, and their own views and preferences third.

Masochistic self-sacrifice is an integral part of most major organized religions: as shown, for example, in the ritualistic self-deprivation that Jews, Christians, and Muslims must continually bear if they are to keep their faith. Orthodox religions deliberately instill guilt (self-damnation) in their adherents and then give these adherents guilt-soothing rituals to (temporarily) allay this kind of self-damning feelings.

Pious secular religionists, instead of bowing to supernatural gods, create semi-divine dictators (for example, Stalin and Hitler) and absolutistic entities (for example, the USSR or the Third Reich) and masochistically demean themselves before these "noble" powers — again to the detriment of their own self-interest.

2. *Self-direction.* Mentally healthy people largely assume responsibility for their own lives, enjoy the independence of mainly

working out their own problems; and, while at times wanting or preferring the help of others, do not think that they absolutely must have such support for their effectiveness and well-being.

Devout religionists (both secular and divine) are almost necessarily dependent and other-directed rather than self-sufficient. To be true to orthodoxies, they first must immolate themselves to their god or god-like hero second to the religious hierarchy that runs their church or organization; and third, to all the other members of their religious sect, who are eagle-eyedly watching them to see if they defect an iota from the conduct that their god and their churchly leadership define as proper.

If devout religiosity, therefore, is often masochism, it is even more often dependency. For humans to be true believers and to also be strong and independent is well nigh impossible. Religiosity and self-sufficiency are contradictory terms.

3. *Social interest*. Emotionally and mentally healthy people are normally gregarious and decide to try to live happily in a social group. Because they want to live successfully with others, and usually to relate intimately to a few of these selected others, they work at feeling and displaying a considerable degree of social interest and interpersonal competence. While they still are primarily interested in their personal survival and enjoyment, they also tend to be considerate and fair to others; to avoid needlessly harming these others; to engage in collaborative and cooperative endeavors; at times to be somewhat altruistic, and to distinctly enjoy some measure of interpersonal and group relationships.

Devout deity-inspired religionists tend to sacrifice human love for godly love (*agape*) and to withdraw into monastic and holy affairs at the expense of intimate interpersonal relationships. They frequently are deficient in social competence. They spend immense amounts of time, effort, and money on establishments rather than on social welfare. They foment religious fights, feuds, wars, and terrorism in the course of which orthodox believers literally batter and kill rather than cooperatively help each other. They encourage charity that is highly parochial and that is linked to god's glory more than to the alleviation of human suffering. Their altruism is highly alloyed with egotistically proving to god how great and glorious they can be as human benefactors.

Devout secular religionists are often much more interested in the propagation of absolutistic creeds (*e.g.*, Maoism) than they are in intimately relating to and in collaboratively helping humans. Like the god-inspired religionists, their charity is exceptionally parochial and is often given only to members of their own religious group while it discriminates against members of groups with opposing credos.

4. *Tolerance*. Emotionally healthy people tend to give other humans the right to be wrong — as I and Dr. Robert A. Harper urged in the original edition of *A New Guide to Rational Living*, which we authored in 1961. While disliking or abhorring others' *behavior*, they refuse to condemn *them*, as total *persons*, for performing their poor behavior. They fully accept the fact that all humans seem to be remarkably fallible; and they refrain from unrealistically demanding and commanding that any of them be perfect; and they desist from damning people *in toto* when they err.

Tolerance is anathema to devout divinity-centered religionists, since they believe that their particular god (*e.g.*, Jehovah or Allah) is absolutely right and that all opposing deities and humans are positively and utterly false and wrong. According to orthodox religious *shalts* and *shalt nots*, you become not only a *wrongdoer* but an arrant *sinner* when you commit ethical and religious misdeeds; and, as a sinner, you become worthless, undeserving of any human happiness, and deserving of being forever damned (excommunicated) on earth and perhaps roasted eternally in hell.

The pious secular religionists, without invoking god or hell, believes that the rules and regulation of his/her group or community (*e.g.* the orthodox religious faction in Iran) are completely right and at the very least, social ostracism, political banishment, and perhaps torture and death should be the lot of any strong dissenter. Religiosity, then, by setting up absolute standards of godly or proper conduct, makes you intolerant of yourself and others when you or they slightly dishonor these standards. Born of this kind of piety-inspired intolerance of self and others come some of the most serious of emotional disorders — such as extreme anxiety, depression, self-hatred, and rage.

5. *Acceptance of ambiguity and uncertainty.* Emotionally mature individuals accept the fact that, as far as has yet been discovered, we live in a world of probability and chance, where there are not, nor probably ever will be absolute necessities or complete certainties. Living in such a world is not only tolerable but in terms of adventure, learning, and striving can even be very exciting and pleasurable.

If one of the requisites for emotional health is acceptance of ambiguity and uncertainty, then divinity-oriented religiosity is the unhealthiest state imaginable, since its prime reason for being is to enable the religionist to believe in god-commanded certainty. Just because life is so uncertain and ambiguous, and because millions of people think that they cannot bear its vicissitudes, they invent absolutistic gods, and thereby pretend that there is some final, invariant answer to human problems. Patently, these people are fooling themselves — and instead of healthfully admitting that they do not need certainty, but can live comfortably in this often disorderly world they stubbornly protect their neurotic beliefs by insisting that there must be the kind of certainty that they wrongly believe they need.

This is like a young boy's believing that he must have a kindly father in order to survive; and then, when his father is unkind, or perhaps has died, the boy dreams up a father (who may be a neighbor, a movie star, or a pure figment of his imagination) and insists that this dream-father actually exists.

Devout secular religionists invent the "certainty" of unequivocally knowing that their special political, economic, social or other creed is indubitably true and cannot be falsified. Like the superhuman-oriented religionists, they also pigheadedly refuse to accept ambiguity and uncertainty — and thereby render and keep themselves neurotically defensive and immature.

6. *Flexibility*. Emotionally sound people are intellectually flexible, tend to be open to change at all times, and are prone to take an unbigoted (or, at least, less bigoted) view of the infinitely varied people, ideas, and things in the world around them. They are not namby-pamby but can be firm and passionate in their thoughts and feelings; but they comfortably look at new evidence and often revise their notions of "reality" to conform with this evidence.

The trait of flexibility, which is so essential to effective emotional functioning, is frequently blocked and sabotaged by profound religiosity. For the person, who dogmatically believes in God, and who sustains this belief with a strong faith unfounded on fact — which a pious religionist of course does — clearly is not open to many aspects of change and, instead, sees things narrowly and bigotedly.

If, for example, a man's scriptures of his church tell him that he shalt not even covet his neighbor's wife — let alone have actual adulterous relations with her! — he cannot ask himself, "Why should I not lust after this woman, as long as I don't intend to do anything about my desire for her? What is really wrong about that?" For his god and his church have spoken; and there is no appeal from this arbitrary authority once he has brought himself to unconditionally accept it.

Any time, in fact, that people unempirically establish a god or a set of religious postulates that supposedly have a super-human origin, they can thereafter use no empirical evidence to question the dictates of this god or those postulates, since they are (by definition) beyond scientific validation. Rigid secular religionists, too, cannot change the rules that their pious creeds establish. Thus, devout Nazis cannot accept any goodness of Jews or of Gypsies, even when it can be incontrovertibly shown that such individuals performed good acts.

The best that devout religionists can do, if they want to change any of the rules that stem from their doctrines, is to change their religion itself. Otherwise, they are stuck with its absolutistic axioms, as well as their logical corollaries that the religionists themselves have initially accepted on faith. We may therefore note again that, just as devout religion is masochism, other-directedness, intolerance, and refusal to accept uncertainty, it also seems to be synonymous with mental and emotional inflexibility.

7. *Scientific thinking.* Emotionally stable people are reasonably (not totally) objective, rational and scientific. They not only construct reasonable and empirically substantiated theories relating to what goes on in the surrounding world (and with their fellow creatures who inhabit this world) but they also, if they follow the teachings of RET, are able to apply the rules of logic and of the scientific method to their own lives and to their interpersonal relationships.

In regard to scientific thinking, it practically goes without saying that this kind of cerebration is antithetical to religiosity. The main requisites of the scientific method — as Bertrand Russell, Ludwig Wittgenstein, Hans Reichenbach, Herbert Feigl, Karl Popper, W.W. Bartley, Michael Mahoney, and a host of other philosophers of science have pointed out — include: (1) At least in some final analysis, or in principle, all scientific theories are to be stated in such a manner that they are confirmable by some form of human experience, by some empirical referents. (2) Scientific theories are those that can in some way be falsified. But deity-oriented religionists contend that the super-human entities that they posit cannot be seen, heard, smelled, tasted, felt, or otherwise humanly experienced and that their gods and their principles are therefore beyond the realm of science. Pious deists and theists believe that the gods or spirits they construct are transcendent: which means, in theology or religion, that they are separate or beyond experience; that they exist apart from the material universe; that, whatever science says they are indubitably true and real.

To devoutly believe in any of the usual religions, therefore, is to be unscientific, and we could well contend that the more devout one is the less scientific one tends to be. Although a pious religionist need not be entirely unscientific (as, for that matter, neither need be a raving maniac), it is difficult to see how such a person could be consistently scientific.

While people may be both scientific and vaguely or generally religious (as, for example many liberal Protestants and reformed Jews tend to be), it is doubtful whether they may simultaneously be thoroughly devout and objective. Devout secular religionists (such as fanatic believers in phrenology or reincarnation) are not necessarily driven to believe in superhuman and supernatural concepts. But they almost inevitably favor absolutistic convictions about certain other issues; and absolutism and dogma are the antithesis of science. Just about all absolutists, secular and godly, tend to flout some of the basic postulates of the scientific method.

8. *Commitment*. As I have noted on several occasions in my writing on rational-emotive therapy (RET), emotionally healthy and happy people are usually absorbed in something outside of themselves, whether this be people, things, or ideas. They seem to lead better lives when they have at least one major creative interest, as well as some outstanding human involvement which they make very important to themselves and around which they structure a good part of their lives.

In regard to the trait of commitment, devoutly religious people may — for once! — have some advantages. For if they are truly religious, and therefore seriously committed to their god, church, or creed, they to some extent acquire a major interest in life. Pious religious commitment, however, frequently has its serious disadvantages, since it tends to be obsessive-compulsive and it may well interfere with other kinds of healthy commitments — such as deep involvements in sex-love relationships, in scientific pursuits, and even in artistic endeavors (because these may interfere with or contradict the religious commitments). Moreover, religious commitment is an absorption that is often motivated by guilt or hostility and that may consequently serve as a frenzied covering-up mechanism that masks, but that does not really eliminate, these underlying disturbed feelings. Pious god-inspired commitment, moreover, is frequently the kind of commitment that is based on falsehoods and illusions and that therefore easily can be shattered, thus plunging the previously committed individual into the depths of disillusionment and despair.

Not all forms of commitment, in other words, are equally healthy or beneficial. The grand inquisitors of the medieval Catholic church were utterly dedicated to their "holy" work and Hitler and many of his associates were fanatically committed to their Nazi doctrines. But this hardly proves that they were emotionally stable humans. In fact, a good case can be made for the proposition that although involved or passionate commitment to some cause or ideal is normally healthy and happiness-producing, devout, pious, or fanatic commitment to the same kind of cause or ideal is potentially pernicious and frequently (though not always) does much more harm than good. Both deity-oriented and secular manifestations of piousness may have distinct advantages for committed individuals. But let us not forget their enormous disadvantages, too!

9. *Risk-taking*. Emotionally sound people are able to take risks, to ask themselves what they would really like to do in life, and then to try to do this, even though they have to risk defeat or failure. They are reasonably adventurous (though not foolhardy); are willing to try almost anything once, if only to see how they like it; and they look forward to some different or unusual breaks in their usual routines.

In regard to risk-taking, I think it is fairly obvious that pious theists are highly determined to avoid adventure and to refuse to take many of life's normal risks. They strongly believe in rigid and unvalidatable assumptions precisely because they are often afraid to follow their own preferences and aims. They demand a guarantee that they will be safe and secure, come what may; and since the real world does not provide them with any such guarantee, they invent some god or other higher power that will presumably give it to them. Their invention of this deity, and their piously subjugating themselves to it, thereby confirms their view that the world is too risky and gives them a further excuse for sticking to inhibiting straight and narrow (and often joyless) paths of existence.

Devout nontheistic religionists mainly substitute dogmatic belief in some philosophy or cause for a fanatical belief in god; and they use this sacredized cause to inhibit themselves against adventure and risk-taking. Thus, pious nutritionists will under no conditions risk eating white bread or sugar, even when it might temporarily do them some good. And devout adherents of cognitive therapy (including devout RETers) may not tolerate the idea that any feeling can be free of thought and will insist that all dysfunctional behaviors (such as headaches and feelings of depression) must be of purely ideological origin.

Enormously fearing failure and rejection, and falsely defining their own worth as humans in terms of achievement and approval, devout religionists sacrifice time, energy, and material goods and pleasures to the worship of their assumed gods or god-like philosophies, so that they can at least be sure that their god loves and supports them or that an inherent Rightness is on their side. All devout religions seem to be distinctly inhibiting — which means, in effect, that piously religious individuals sell their soul, surrender their own basic urges and pleasures, in order to feel comfortable with the heavenly helper or the indubitably correct creed that they have invented or adopted. Religiosity, then, importantly consists of needless, self-defeating inhibition.

10. *Self-acceptance*. People who are emotionally healthy are usually glad to be alive and to accept themselves as "deserving" of continued life and of happiness just because they exist and because they have some present or future potential to enjoy themselves. In accordance with the principles of RET they *fully* or *unconditionally* accept themselves (or give themselves what Carl Rogers calls

unconditionally positive regard). They try to perform adequately or competently in their affairs and to win the approval and love of others; but they do so for enjoyment and not for ego gratification or for self-deification. They consequently try to rate only their acts, deeds, and traits, in the light of the goals, values, and purposes they choose (such as the goals of graduating from school or of having an enjoyable sex-love relationship); and they rigorously try to avoid rating their *self*, their *being*, their *essence*, or their *totality*.

Healthy people, in other words, unconditionally accept themselves because they *choose* to do so, regardless of how well or badly they perform and regardless of how much approval they receive from others. They distinctly *prefer* to act competently and to win others' favor and they accordingly assess and criticize their own *behaviors* when they fail in these respects. But they don't hold that they absolutely *must* do well or be loved; and they therefore don't conclude that *they*, *in toto*, are good *people* when they succeed and are rotten *individuals* when they fail.

In regard to self-acceptance, it seems clear that devout religionists cannot accept themselves just because they are alive and because they have some power to enjoy life. Rather, orthodox theists make their self-acceptance quite contingent on their being accepted by the god, the church, the clergy, and the other members of the religious denomination in which they believe. If all these extrinsic persons and things accept them, then and then only are they able to accept themselves. Which means that these religionists define themselves only through the reflected appraisals of god and of other humans. Fanatical religion, for such individuals, almost necessarily winds up with lack of unconditional self-acceptance and, instead, with a considerable degree of self-abasement and self-abnegation — as, of course, virtually all the saints and mystics have found.

What about theistic religions, like Christianity, that presumably give grace to all people who accept their tenets and thereby allow all humans to accept themselves unconditionally? As far as I know, there are no theistic creeds that actually do this. The best of them — like Science of Mind — state that god (or Jesus) is all-loving and that s/he therefore always gives everyone grace or unconditional acceptance. But these theistic religions still require their adherents to believe (1) that a God (or son of god) must exist; (2) that s/he personally gives you unconditional acceptance or grace; and (3) that consequently you must believe in this religion and in its god to receive the "unconditional" grace. Unless you accept these three *conditions* of grace, you will presumably never be fully self-accepting. And these *conditions*, of course, make your accepting of yourself *conditional* rather than *un*-conditional. Nonreligious philosophies, such as RET, teach that you can always choose to accept yourself just *because* you decide to do so, and require no conditions or redundant beliefs in god or religion to help you do this choosing.

Ironically, in fact, when you do decide to adopt a religious view and choose to accept yourself conditionally (because you believe in a grace-giving god or son-of-god), *you* choose to believe in this religion and *you* consequently create the grace-giver who "makes" you self-acceptable. All religiously-inspired forms of self-acceptance, therefore, in the final analysis depend on *your* belief system; and they are consequently actually self-inspired! Even when a religion supposedly "gives" you grace, you really *choose* it yourself, and the religious trappings in which you frame your self-acceptance consist of a redundant hypothesis (that God exists and that s/he gives you grace) that is utterly unprovable and unfalsifiable and that really adds nothing to your *own* decision to be self-accepting.

Although liberal religionists (like the followers of Science of Mind) may be largely self-accepting, devout religionists have much more trouble in gaining any measure of unconditional self-acceptance. This goes for devout secular as well as pious theistic believers. For the former cannot unconditionally accept themselves because they invariably seem to make self-acceptance (or, worse yet, ego-inflation or self-esteem) depend on their adhering rigidly to the tenets of their particular creed. Thus, fanatical Nazis only see themselves (and others) as good *people* if they are good Nazis; and if they perform non-Nazi or anti-Nazi acts (*e.g.*, espouse internationalism or help Jews or Gypsies) they damn themselves as rotten *individuals*, who presumably deserve to suffer and die. Ku Klux Klanners, along with downing Blacks, Jews, Catholics, and others, excoriate *themselves* as worthless when they fail to live up to ideal KKK standards. Pious secular religionists, like fanatical theists, seem incapable of unconditionally accepting themselves (or others), since one of the essences of devoutness or fanaticism is to thoroughly damn and to attempt to censor and punish all those who even mildly disagree with the fanatics view.

A special way in which devout religiosity sabotages unconditional self-acceptance is its strong tendency to encourage ego-aggrandizing or grandiosity. It is clearly self-defeating to tell yourself, "I am a good person because I have good character," or "I can esteem myself because I am highly competent." For if you give yourself this kind of ego-bolstering you make yourself highly liable to self-downing as soon as it can be shown that your character is not so good or that you are beginning, in some important way, to act incompetently.

You will do even worse if you make such self statements as, "I am a great or noble person because I do outstandingly well at work or at art," or "Because I subscribe to this particular fine philosophy or cause I am better than you are and am indeed a superior individual!" For this kind of holier-than-thou self-rating, or arrant grandiosity, assumes that you and other people can be truly superior and godlike — and that you and they are thoroughly ordinary or worthless when they are not looking down from some kind of heavenly perch.

Devout religiosity particularly foments ego bolstering and grandiosity. Where mild religionists think of themselves as good people because they are members in good standing of their own religious group, pious ones frequently think of themselves as utterly noble and great because of their religious convictions. Thus, pious Christians, Jews, fascists, and communists tend to deify themselves for their beliefs and allegiances; and probably devout Atheists also tend to feel somewhat god-like and holy! Grandiosity is one of the most common of human disturbed feelings; and it often compensates for underlying feelings of slobhood. In fact, as Camilla Anderson, a notably sane psychiatrist, has shown, few of us would ever wind up feeling like turds if we did not start off with the grandiose assumptions that we must — yes, *must* — be noble and great.

Anyway, devout religionists are frequently attracted to and bound to their piety largely because it presumably offers them holier-than-thou-ness and, one-upmanship over non-religionists. And by its appeal to such disturbed individuals, devout religious creeds encourage some of the craziest kinds of thoughts, emotions and behaviors and favor severe manifestations of neurosis, borderline personality states, and sometimes even psychosis.

11. Emotionally healthy people, it almost goes without saying, accept WIGO (what is going on) in the world. This means several important things: (1) They have a reasonably good perception of reality and do not see things that do not exist and do not refuse to see things that do. (2) They find various aspects of reality, in accordance with their own goals and inclination, "good" and certain aspects "bad" — but they accept both these aspects, without exaggerating the "good" realities and without denying or whining about the "bad" ones. (3) They do their best to work at changing those aspects of reality that they view as "bad", to accept those that they cannot change, and to acknowledge the difference between the two.

Devout theistic religionists frequently refuse to accept reality in all three of the ways just listed: (1) They are frequently sure that they see things — *e.g.*, gods, angels, devils, and absolute laws of the universe — for which there is no confirmatory empirical data and that in all probability do not actually exist. And they refuse to see some obvious things — such as the ubiquity of human fallibility and the overwhelming unlikelihood that any humans will ever be perfect — that almost certainly do exist. (2) They often whine and scream — and even have their gods whine and scream (as Jehovah presumably did when he turned Lot's wife into a pillar of salt for looking back at Sodom and Gomorrah) when they see something "bad." They especially indulge in childish whining and in temper tantrums when other religionists or non-believers refuse to see the virtues of the devout theists' favored religious dogmas. (3) Instead of working hard to change grim reality, they often pray to their god(s) to bring about such changes while they impotently sit on their rumps waiting for their prayers to be answered. When certain obvious things are unchangeable — such as the propensity of humans to become ill and to die — they refuse to accept these realities and often invent utopian heavens where humans presumably live forever in perfect bliss, without their suffering any kinds of affliction. Obviously, therefore, devout theists often ignore, deny, and hallucinate about reality; and the more devout they are — as the long history of religion shows — the more delusionary and hallucinatory they seem to be.

Devout nontheistic religionists — such as orthodox and closed-minded capitalists, communists, and rationalists — rarely seem to deny reality as much as do devout theists. But because they dogmatically and absolutistically follow narrow creeds, they frequently look at the world and the people in it with heavily Pollyannaish and/or overly pessimistic glasses and they thereby significantly distort reality by seeing it in enormously wishful-thinking ways.

If we summarize what we have been saying, the conclusion seems inescapable that religiosity is, on almost every conceivable count, opposed to the normal goals of mental health. Instead, it encourages masochism, other-directedness, social withdrawal, intolerance, refusal to accept ambiguity and uncertainty, unscientific thinking, needless inhibition, lack of self-acceptance, and reluctance to acknowledge and deal adequately with reality. In the one area where devout religion has some advantage — that of encouraging commitment to a cause or project in which people may become vitally absorbed — it even tends to sabotage this advantage in two important ways: (1) It encourages its adherents to commit themselves to its tenets for the wrong reasons — that is, to cover up instead of to face and rid themselves of their personal insecurities. (2) It encourages a fanatic, obsessive-compulsive kind of commitment that is, in its own right, a form of emotional disturbance.

This is not to deny that for some people some of the time religious notions, even when they are devoutly and rigidly held, have some benefits. Of course they do. Devout adherence to a theistic or secular form of religion can at times motivate people to help others who are needy to give up unhealthy addictions (*e.g.* to cigarettes or alcohol), to follow valuable disciplines (*e.g.* dieting or exercising), to go for psychotherapy, to strive for world peace, to follow long-range instead of short-range hedonism, and to work for many other kinds of valuable goals. Historical and biographical data abound to show this good side of religiosity. But I would still contend that on the whole religious piety and dogma do much more harm than good; and the beneficent behaviors that they sometimes abet would most likely be more frequent and profound without their influence.

As a good case in point, let us take the issue of interpersonal and political war and peace. Unquestionably, many devout religionists (*e.g.* St. Francis and St. Theresa) have led notably unangry and loving existences themselves and many others (*e.g.*, several of the popes) have helped in the creation of world peace. So pious religion and surcease from human aggression hardly are completely incompatible. The fact remains, however, that fanaticism of any kind, especially religious fanaticism, has clearly produced and in all probability will continue to produce enormous amounts of bickering, fighting, violence, bloodshed, homicide, feuds, wars, and genocide.

For all its peace-inviting potential, therefore, arrant (not to mention arrogant) religiosity has led to immense individual and social harm by fomenting an incredible amount of antihuman and antihumane aggression. It can therefore be concluded that anger-attacking and peace-loving religious views that are held undevoutly and unrigidly, as well as similar views that are held by nonreligionists and antireligionists, probably serve humankind far better than religiosity-inspired peace efforts.

Religion, then, is not all bad; and even devout religiosity has some saving graces. But on the whole and in the main? The legacy and the future of dogmatic religion seem to be indicative of considerably more human harm than good.

If religiosity is so inimical to mental health and happiness, what are the chances of unbelief, skepticism, and thoroughgoing Atheism helping humans in this important aspect of their lives? I would say excellent. My own view — based on more than forty years of research and clinical work in the field of psychology and psychotherapy but still admittedly prejudiced by my personal predilections and feelings — is that if people were thoroughly unbelieving of any dogmas, if they were highly skeptical of all hypotheses and theories that they formulated, if they believed in no kinds of gods, devils, or other supernatural beings, and if they subscribed to no forms of absolutistic thinking, they would be minimally emotionally disturbed and maximally healthy. Stated a little differently: if you, I, and everyone else in the world were thoroughly scientific, and if we consistently used the scientific method in our own lives and in our relationships with others, we would rarely upset ourselves about anything — and I mean *anything*!

My view of the incompatibility of skepticism and scientific thinking with what we usually call neurosis or emotional upsetness stems from my work with rational-emotive therapy (RET), a leading school of modern psychotherapy, which I founded at the beginning of 1955, after I had become disillusioned with practicing psychoanalysis and several other modes of therapy. RET is a comprehensive or multimodal system, which investigates the cognitive, emotive, and behavioral origins of human disturbance and that therefore employs a large variety of thinking, feeling, and activity-oriented methods of understanding and alleviating this disturbance. It is most famous, however, for its cognitive or philosophic theories and practices and is the father of what is now often called cognitive or cognitive behavior therapy.

One of the main postulates of RET is that neurotic disorder largely (but not completely) stems, not from the situations or events that happen to people in their past or present lives but from their own thinking *about* these events — from the explicit and implicit ideas, attitudes, philosophies, and self-statements that they believe just prior to feeling emotionally upset. Thus, when people feel anxious, depressed, inadequate, angry or self-pitying, they feel these ways because they almost invariably tell themselves, *and devoutly believe*, one or more irrational or self-defeating ideas. I first outlined, in my original paper on RET that I presented at the American Psychological Association convention in Chicago in 1956, ten major irrational (that is, antiempirical and illogical) beliefs that people strongly hold when they upset themselves. But I later found that these can be reduced to three basic irrationalities — and that, coincidentally enough, all three of these consist of absolutistic shoulds, oughts, and musts.

I found what Karen Horney had discovered a decade before I originated RET: that human disturbance largely comes from what she called *the tyranny of the shoulds* — or from what I call *must*-urbation. Whenever people feel distinctly anxious, depressed, hostile, self-pitying, or otherwise needlessly neurotic, whenever they behave distinctly against their own wishes and interests (as when they are addicted to procrastination, smoking, or drinking even though they very much want to forego these self-defeating behaviors), they seem to devoutly believe, explicitly and/or implicitly, one or more of these *must*-urbatory creeds: (1) "I *must* perform well and *have to* win the approval of significant others by doing so, else it's *awful* and I am a *worthless person!*" (2) "Other people *must* treat me fairly and considerately; and if they don't it's *terrible* and they are *rotten individuals!*" (3) Conditions under which I live *must* be nice and comfortable and absolutely *should* easily provide me with what I want; else life is *horrible*, I *can't stand* it, and I might just as well be dead!"

If people did not consciously and unconsciously believe any of these absolutistic, unconditional musts, shoulds, and oughts, RET clearly hypothesizes, they would feel *appropriately* sad, regretful, frustrated, and annoyed when their desires and preferences are not fulfilled. But they would rarely, if ever, feel *in*-appropriately panicked, despairing, self-downing, enraged, or self-pitying. Stated differently: if humans only *strongly preferred*, *wished*, or *desired* goals and things that they favored and only *wanted* to avoid things they disfavored, and if they never Jehovianly *demanded*, *commanded*, or *necessitated* that the situations they viewed as "good" exist and those they viewed as "bad" not exist, they would not seriously disturb themselves about anything — including failure, rejection, injustice, disaster, and death. Instead, they would resolutely encounter such disadvantageous conditions; feel appropriately sad (but not horrified) about them; feel strongly determined to alleviate or eliminate them; and unwhiningly accept them when they could not change these conditions.

Assuming (as RET does) that most of what we call emotional disturbance stems from absolutistic thinking — from unconditional and dogmatic shoulds, oughts, and musts that we tell ourselves and devoutly believe — what are the main ways to change this kind of thinking and to train ourselves to live with desires and preferences instead of with godlike commands on ourselves, on others, and on the universe? RET uses many cognitive, emotive, and behavioral methods of doing this — as I have explained in several of my books, such as *Reason and Emotion in Psychotherapy, Growth Through Reason, Humanistic Psychotherapy:*

the *Rational-Emotive Approach, Handbook of Rational-Emotive Therapy*, and *Rational-Emotive Therapy and Cognitive Behavior Therapy*. Probably the most elegant and thoroughgoing of these RET methods is that of Disputing — which has also at times been called cognitive restructuring, cognitive therapy, selfinstructional training, semantic therapy, and the use of coping statements. In RET, Disputing is synonymous with skepticism, unbelief, and the scientific method. It consists of taking your basic irrational Beliefs (iBs) or your absolutistic hypotheses about yourself, others, and the world, and actively and forcefully questioning and challenging these Beliefs, until you thoroughly surrender them and replace them with rational Beliefs (rBs).

Let me briefly explain the RET Disputing process. Suppose that at point A (Activating Event) you try for a very good job that you greatly desire, mess up during the interview process, and get rejected for the job. At point C (Consequence) you feel neurotically depressed and withdraw from all further job-seeking efforts. If you know the principles of RET, you realize that although A (Activating Event consisting of failure and rejection) contributes to C (Consequence of depression and withdrawal) it does not directly "cause" it. The more important "cause" of C is B — your Beliefs about what has transpired at A. So you look, first for your desires or rational Beliefs (rBs) and soon find them to be: "I wish I had succeeded and got accepted for this good job, and since I failed that's quite unfortunate and frustrating. But because this isn't the only good job I might get, it isn't the end of the world. Too bad! Now let me keep looking until I get another job that I really want." You see that if you rigorously and only stick to this set of rational Beliefs (rBs) you would feel appropriately sad and frustrated — but not inappropriately and neurotically depressed and withdrawn.

You therefore, still using RET, look for your irrational Beliefs (iBs) — knowing (on theoretical grounds) that they are absolutistic and unrealistic (antiempirical). Since they usually follow similar patterns, you quickly find these irrational Beliefs: (1) "I absolutely *should* not, *must* not have failed as I did in seeking this good job!" (2) How *awful* for me to fail (as I *must* not have done) and get rejected!" (3) "I *can't stand* failing and being rejected (4) Because I failed and got rejected for this job (as I *must* not have done) and because there *must* be something radically wrong with me for failing, I am an *inadequate person* who will doubtless fall at getting all other good jobs; who is undeserving, in fact, of getting any really good one; and who might as well quit trying to better my position in life!"

After discovering, through the use of RET, the ABCs of your feelings and depression, inadequacy, and withdrawal when you have failed to get a job that you greatly wanted, and later clearly seeing that the As (Activating Events) contribute to the Cs (disturbed emotional and behavioral Consequences) but not directly "cause" them, and after realizing, instead that your iBs (irrational Beliefs about the As) more directly and importantly lead to these Cs, you then proceed to D (the Disputing of your irrational Beliefs). D (Disputing) is another name for skepticism, scientific thinking, unbelief, and the logico-empirical method of extirpating antiempirical or unrealistic dogmas. Using Disputing (or the scientific method), you vigorously challenge and eliminate your irrational Beliefs (iBs) as follows:

1. You ask yourself: "Where is the evidence that I absolutely *should* not, *must* not have failed as I did in seeking this good job?" Answer: "There is no evidence for my *should* or *must*. It probably would have been highly preferable if I had succeeded in getting this job (though it is possible, also, that it would not have been preferable but turned out badly.) But no matter how *preferable* it would have been, there is no *necessity* for my preferences to be fulfilled. There is no law of the universe that says that because I greatly *want* something it *must* be granted to me. If such a law existed, then I *would have* got the job; so obviously this law does not exist. Unconditional necessities — *e.g.*, my having to have what

I distinctly desire — may be *my* law, but the world clearly does not include this rule! If I *must* not have failed to get this job, then I obviously would have got it. But, clearly, I didn't! Therefore my *must* is contradicted by reality, and I had better change it back into a strong preference."

2. You ask yourself: "In what way is it *awful* or *terrible* for me to fail and get rejected for this highly desirable job?" Answer: "In no way!" Obviously, it is distinctly unpleasant and inconvenient for me to be rejected when I really want this job. But *awful* and *terrible* do not merely mean *unpleasant* or even *very unpleasant*. *Awful* means, over and above *inconvenient*, that it is *totally* bad 100% *annoying* that I failed to get this job. But that is most unlikely, since only something like being crippled for life or being dead would be close to 100% bad. And even *that* wouldn't really be 100% bad — since I can think of things worse than that, such as being crippled for life and being in continual pain. *Awful* or *terrible* means, second, *more than* bad, *more than* completely obnoxious — but, of course, nothing that ever happens to me could be more than 100% bad! *Awful* means, third, badder than it *should* or *must* be. But however bad it is for me to lose this job, it *must* be exactly that bad — for that's the way it is! So whenever I tell myself that anything is *awful, terrible,* or *horrible* I am really going beyond reality and contending that just because I really don't like it, and even greatly deplore it, it *must* not exist. What rot! Whatever exists exists! — no matter how bad I personally find it.!

3. You ask yourself: "Is it really true that I *can't stand* losing this job and getting rejected?" Answer: "Of course I can stand it! I may never *like* it; I may, in fact, *enormously abhor* this loss and rejection. But I can always *stand* what I don't like, unless it is literally lethal and kills me. Even then, I can stand it till I die! Thus, if a steam roller rolls over me and kills me, it is silly to tell myself, while I am still alive, 'I *can't stand* it, I *can't stand it!*' — for that is exactly what I am doing until I am literally dead standing it, bearing it. The term, 'I can't stand

it!' really has no sense to it, since as long as I (or anyone else) lives, we *have* to stand whatever goes on in our lives, whether it be injustice, torture, or anything else. Only when we are dead does the phrase make any sense. And when, while still alive and kicking, I whine and scream, 'I *can't stand* being rejected for this job!' I am obviously out of my foolish head. For I *am* standing it. Even if I kill myself because I lost this job, I am still *deciding* to do so and the loss of the job itself does not *make me* do so. It is not because I can't stand it that I kill myself but because I idiotically *think* I can't stand it — when, of course, I really can. So I'd better almost completely eliminate the phrases, 'I can't stand it!' or 'I can't bear it' from my thinking and my vocabulary since they are virtually never in accordance with reality."

4. You ask yourself, "Where is it written that there must be something radically wrong with me for failing to get this job? And even if it can be shown that there is something seriously wrong with me, and that I will therefore lose other good jobs as well, where is the evidence that (a) I am an *inadequate person* who will doubtless fail at getting *all* other good jobs; (b) I am therefore undeserving of ever getting any fine position; and (c) I therefore might as 'well quit trying to better my position in life?" Answer: "All these ideas are only written in my deluded head. First, I can easily fail to get this job or other good jobs when there is nothing radically wrong with me, but for several other reasons (such as the competition's being very heavy or my potential bosses not wanting to hire me because I am *too* intelligent or *too* competent). Second, even if it can be shown that there is something radically wrong with me, that merely means that I am a *person who has inadequacies* and not an *inadequate person*. For an inadequate person would always and only have inadequacies; and it is most unlikely that my traits are universally that bad. Third, even if I frequently act quite inadequately and incompetently, that never proves that I am *undeserving* of ever getting any fine position and that some universal law of *deservingness* will absolutely prevent me from getting one. It merely proves

that, statistically speaking, the probability of my getting the kind of position that I want is rather low, but that if I keep trying very hard I might well finally get it.

If you Dispute, and keep Disputing, your irrational Beliefs (iBs) in this manner, the theory and practice of RET says that you will rarely feel emotionally disturbed and will seldom foolishly act against your own interests; and when you do, you will quickly be able to see what you are doing to needlessly upset yourself and will be able to 'un-upset' yourself again. But let me repeat, so that there will be little misunderstanding about this! — RET does not show you how to be completely calm, serene, detached, unfeeling, passive, or resigned. As its name implies, it is a rational-*emotive* type of therapy; and it assumes that you, like practically all humans, strongly desire to remain alive and to be happy. It therefore, in many ways, helps you feel *more* than you normally would — but to feel pleasure, joy, elation, and occasional ecstasy when things are going the way you want them to go and to feel, and sometimes strongly feel, sorrow, regret, frustration, and annoyance when you are not getting what you would really want to get out of life.

The Disputing that you do when you use RET is synonymous with the scientific method of challenging or disputing unrealistic or invalid hypotheses; and it is the same kind of skepticism and unbelief that you would use if you were desirous of uprooting your (or anyone else's) devout religiosity. RET, therefore, when it is employed in the manner in which I and my close associates employ it, is equivalent to the scientific method and is one of the most powerful foes of religious piety, fanaticism, and dogma.

To sum up what I have been saying in this essay: Vague, general, or mild "religion" seems to consist of people's having some serious philosophy of life, and especially an outlook about important questions like those of ethics, death, immortality, and the origin, development, and outcome of the universe. It is sometimes (and sometimes not) connected with a belief in superhuman sources and powers. This kind of religion seems a natural part of the human condition and does not seem to be intrinsically connected to mental health: since it has not been shown that vague religionists — whether they be theists, pantheists, or humanists — are emotionally healthier or unhealthier than nonreligionists. In fact, if we talk only about vague or moderate forms of "religion" it is not clear that any thoroughgoing "nonreligionists" even exist!

Devout or pious religionists, or devotees of religiosity, seem to be distinctly different from mild religionists in that they hold to their beliefs in a distinctly dogmatic, orthodox, absolutistic, rigid, closed manner. Many of them are devoutly or piously theistic — *e.g.*, orthodox Jews, Catholics, Protestants, Muslims, or mystics — and therefore worship divine or superhuman power(s). But many of them are devout secular religionists — *e.g.*, fanatical communists, Nazis, liberationists, or rightwing or leftwing terrorists — who are largely or completely non-theistic. Devout theistic and devout secular religionists differ in some important ways; but in regard to their fanaticism and absolutism they are remarkably similar.

It is my contention that both pietistic theists and secular religionists — like virtually all people imbued with intense religiosity and fanaticism are emotionally disturbed: usually neurotic and sometimes psychotic. For they strongly and rigidly believe in the same kinds of profound irrationalities, absolutistic musts, and unconditional necessities in which seriously disturbed people powerfully believe. When, moreover, they employ the logico-empirical methods of science, and when they fully accept (while often distinctly disliking and actively trying to change) reality, they are able to surrender their devoutness and to become significantly less disturbed. Indeed, I hypothesize, the more scientific, open-minded, and straight-thinking about themselves, about others, and about the world people are, the less neurotically they will think, feel and behave. This is my major hypothesis about the relationship between absolutistic religious belief (religiosity) and mental health. The evidence that I have found, clinically and experimentally, in support of this hypothesis (as well as the evidence falsifying the hypothesis that devout religiosity is significantly correlated with and probably causative of good mental health) seems to be most impressive. But much more investigation of this issue had better be done, since it is up to me and others to empirically bolster or disconfirm these hypotheses.

REFERENCES

Adler, A. *Understanding Human Nature*. New York: Garden City Publishing Company, 1927.

Anderson, C.A. "Depression and suicide reassessed." *Journal of the American Medicine Woman's Association*, June 1964, 1–7.

Bartley, W.W. "Theories of demaraction between science and metaphysics." In I. Lakatos and A. Musgrave (Eds.), *Problems in the Philosophy of Science*. Amsterdam: North Holland Publishing Company, 1968.

Dreikurs, R. *Psychodynamics, Psychotherapy and Counseling*. Chicago: Alfred Adler Institute, 1974.

Ellis, A. *How to Live with a "Neurotic"*. New York: Crown, 1957. Rev. ed., New York: Crown, 1975.

Ellis, A. *Reason and Emotion in Psychotherapy*. Secaucus, N.J.: Lyle Stuart and Citadel Press, 1962.

Ellis, A. *Growth through Reason*. Palo Alto: Science and Behavior Books and Hollywood: Wilshire Books, 1971.

Ellis, A. *Humanistic Psychotherapy: The Rational-Emotive Approach*. New York: Crown and McGraw-Hill Paperbacks, 1973.

Ellis, A. *Rational-Emotive Therapy and Cognitive Behavior Therapy*. In press.

Ellis, A., & Grieger, R. (Eds.) *Handbook of Rational-Emotive Therapy*. New York: Springer, 1977.

Ellis, A., & Harper, R.A. *New Guide to Rational Living.* Englewood Cliffs, N.J.: Prentice-hall and Hollywood: Wilshire Books, 1975.

Feigl, H. *Operationism and Scientific Method. Psychological Review,* 1945, 52, 250–259.

Freud, S. *Standard Edition of the Complete Psychological Works of Sigmund Freud.* New York: Basic Books, 1965.

Fromm, E. *Escape from Freedom.* New York Rinehart, 1941.

Horney, K. *Collected Works.* New York: Norton, 1965.

Jahoda, M. "What is prejudice?" *World Mental Health,* 1961, 13 38–45.

Jung, C. G. *The Practice of Psychotherapy.* New York: Pantheon,1954.

Mahoney, M. *Scientist as Subject: The Psychological Imperative.* Cambridge, Mass.: Ballinger, 1976.

Maslow, A. *Motivation and Personality.* Rev. ed. New York: Harper, 1970.

May, R. *Love and Will.* New York: Norton, 1969.

Perls, F. *Gestalt Therapy Verbatim.* Lafayette, Calif.: Real People Press, 1969.

Popper, K. *Objective Knowledge.* London: Oxford, 1972.

Reichenbach, H. "The verifiability theory in meaning." In H. Feigl and M. Brodbeck (eds.), *Readings in the Philosophy of Science.* New York: Appleton-Century-Crofs, 1953.

Rogers, C. *On Becoming a Person.* Boston: Houghton Mifflin, 1961.

Russell, B. *The Basic Writings of Bertrand Russell.* New York: Simon and Schuster, 1961.

Wittgenstein, L. *Philisophical Investigations.* New York: Macmillan, 1958.